Tracking Down the True Church

Karl Keating

RASSELAS
HOUSE

Published by Rasselas House
El Cajon, California
RasselasHouse.com

Cover design by EbookLaunch.com
Formatting by PolgarusStudio.com

ISBN 978-1-942596-23-3 Paperback
ISBN 978-1-942596-22-6 Ebook

Contents

Introduction

We drove up to the high school campus. There was a small parking lot between us and the gymnasium, where the debate would be held. "Looks like we have competition from a football game," I said. Yellow buses were pulling into the lot, spilling passengers into a large crowd of people milling around on the grass. We turned in behind a bus, and I hit the brakes. Now we were close enough to see the unsmiling faces. Everyone was dressed in Sunday-go-to-meetin' clothes. "I don't think they're here for football," said my co-worker.

"What's going on? The debate isn't for two-and-a-half hours. Where have all these people come from?" They were coming from all over Southern California, expecting to see their hero, a minister for Iglesia ni Cristo ("Church of Christ" in Tagalog), rhetorically smash a Catholic apologist. I was to be the smashee.

We parked the van and walked to the gymnasium. Iglesia men in three-piece suits were speaking into walkie-talkies. Several women were setting up a reception table outside the foyer. Others were checking off names on long lists. At the side door trucks filled with folding chairs were being unloaded. Farther back, people were taking video equipment out of a van. And behind us more yellow buses were pulling into the lot, disgorging passengers, and moving on.

We walked inside, stepped over cables, dodged men carrying chairs. Against the wall opposite the foyer was the raised platform: lecterns, tables, microphones, and, off to the left, an overhead projector and large screen. Video cameras were being set up in a semicircle in front of the platform. Technicians hovered around them, armed with bandoliers of battery packs.

The bleachers had been extended on both sides of the gymnasium. The floor was being filled rapidly with folding chairs, some of which already had been claimed. Several dozen impeccably dressed Iglesia members wore badges identifying themselves as ushers. They greeted people at the doors and took them to seats that seemed to be assigned. The mood of the audience was distressingly expectant, perhaps not unlike the mood of audiences at a Roman arena. These people were looking for blood—mine.

After we set up a book table (we ended up selling almost nothing since Iglesia people are discouraged from reading anything but their own church's literature), I started to look for my opponent, Jose Ventilacion, the minister from the National City, California, Church of Christ. His church is visible from the freeway and gets plenty of stares—and with good reason. Iglesia churches are reminiscent of Mormon temples. They feature multiple pinnacled towers (though none with a trumpet-blowing angel Moroni on top). Some people say the architecture reminds them of the Emerald City in the *Wizard of Oz*. In the Philippines it is said the Iglesia churches are built not so much with an eye to aesthetics but with an eye to necessity.

At the rapture, or so the story goes, Iglesia members will be whooshed into heaven, but only if they're inside one of their churches when the rapture comes. The church building too will be taken up, thus the need for the aerodynamic design. The story may be apocryphal, but I wouldn't dismiss it out of hand. These people believe strange things, and they believe them sincerely—more than sincerely, fanatically. Their fanaticism is not to be taken lightly.

When I sat down at my place on the platform, an Iglesia man took a chair a few feet away, near the stairs. "What are you doing?" I asked.

"I'm your bodyguard," he said. "At our debates in the Philippines, people often charge the platform, and I'm here to protect you in case that happens." I was not comforted. What good would one bodyguard be against 3,500 people trained to hate Catholicism?

I should give a little background about this strange sect. Its founder was Felix Manalo. Baptized a Catholic, he fell away from the Church as a teenager. Later he was influenced by Protestant missionaries who had come to the Philippines. He also must have been influenced by Mormons and Jehovah's Witnesses, since his church's distinctive doctrines seem taken from those religions.

In 1914 Manalo incorporated Iglesia ni Cristo in the Philippines. Within a few years he was teaching that the Christian Church had apostatized in the first century and had ceased to exist. Eighteen-and-a-half centuries later, God instructed Manalo to effect a restoration. Today's head of Iglesia ni Cristo is Manalo's grandson, Eduardo.

The church publishes a monthly magazine. At the time of the debate it was called *Pasugo*, but nowadays, to appeal to people who don't speak Tagalog, it is called *God's Message.* Its most notable feature is its strident and low-brow anti-Catholicism. It is also anti-Protestant. The Catholic and Protestant churches, but especially the former, are tools of Satan, say the writers. Each issue has more pages devoted to debunking Christian churches than to explaining Iglesia's own positions. In a way that's understandable: Iglesia ni Cristo has few positions to explain. This is a sect built not so much on doctrines but on anti-doctrines. The members are told what to shun; there isn't much for them to accept in the positive sense.

Unlike Fundamentalism, unlike even Mormonism and the Jehovah's Witnesses, Iglesia ni Cristo is a true cult. If you had seen the Iglesia people in the audience, if you had seen how they reacted in lock-step to their leaders, you would have understood that. At least that's the impression I got, from my vantage point on the platform.

The gymnasium was preternaturally hot. An hour before the start of the debate the people seated on the folding chairs were fanning themselves. At the top of the bleachers it was hotter still. And on the platform, under the klieg lights, it was hellish. (I went through a quart of water before the night was over.) I wondered if someone had turned on the heaters in the afternoon of this balmy early October day, in order to get the audience on edge. I wouldn't doubt it. The Iglesia folks are sneaky.

Jose Ventilacion and I had negotiated terms of the debate over a period of several months. Each time a change was made in the format, he had to check with authorities in Manila. I had been warned by people who had seen Iglesia debates not to trust Ventilacion. I pooh-poohed the warnings, but I was wrong. The terms of the debate were broken even before I arrived at the gymnasium.

Ventilacion and I had agreed this would be *mano-a-mano*, just the two of us. I was seated alone at my table, but he had two "seconds" at his. Their job was to pass him notes and books to read from while he was at the lectern. Sometimes they did more than that. One of them, himself a minister, was unable to control himself during my remarks. He repeatedly stood up and shouted at me. "I'm not debating you," I shouted back. "I'm debating *him*. Sit down!" (This and other irrelevant exchanges have been edited out of the transcript that follows.)

The overhead projector also wasn't part of the agreement. It was placed on Ventilacion's side of the platform, with two more of his people manning it. When I first saw it and realized that its operators would be acting as yet more helpers, I complained to Ventilacion. He flashed a toothy smile. "If you don't agree to this format, we'll cancel the debate and give our people an instruction." By that he meant he'd just preach to them.

I didn't have much choice. The listeners were mainly former Catholics bamboozled by Iglesia ni Cristo's anti-Catholic rhetoric. They *needed* to hear what the Catholic Church really stood for—and what *their* church really stood for and how it came to be. Besides, five against one had a positive aspect. I was bound to get a certain amount of sympathy, especially if I explained the situation—which I did. But Ventilacion, in the question period following my opening remarks, said I misrepresented the facts, that I had "agreed" to the format. I replied, "If you say, 'If you don't give me your money, I'll shoot you,' of course I'll give you my money." Ventilacion said I shouldn't worry about technicalities, but it was clear *his* people had spent *lots* of time worrying about technicalities. You don't produce a well-orchestrated (well-railroaded?) debate by ignoring the little things.

However meticulous it may be organizationally, Iglesia ni Cristo is remarkably cavalier when it comes to "the little things" of theology. Its positions are just stated, never really substantiated. Its arguments are puerile. For instance, believers in the claims of Felix Manalo say Revelation's references to an "angel" coming out of the "East" or from "afar" refer to a "messenger" ("angel" is taken from the Greek for "messenger") coming from the "Far East." And what is the geographic center of the Far East? Why, the Philippines, of course. Therefore, Felix Manalo was a true prophet: (1) he claimed to be a prophet, which means (2) that he claimed to be God's messenger, and (3) he came from the Far East.

How to respond to such a claim? I started by listing the countries that make up the Far East: China, Korea, Japan, Taiwan, Hong Kong, Indochina, and, yes, the Philippines. "If you look at a map of the Far East," I said, "you'll see that the Philippines is in the southeast corner." The geographic center is in southern China, not in the Philippines. There were laughs from the Catholics and Protestants (a few hundred of them were in the audience), nervous fidgeting from the Iglesia people.

Later on, after having dealt with the main charges against the Catholic Church, I zeroed in on Manalo himself. Iglesia ni Cristo tells its members little about their founder: what I said brought a strange silence to the gymnasium. I explained Manalo's early years and how, as it is now said, he began his church in 1914 after receiving a revelation from God and being informed that he was the new prophet. I asked the audience why, five years later in 1919, did Manalo go to the U.S. to study with Protestants? Why would he study with people he later claimed were "apostates"? Why would a prophet need to study religion at all, after having talked with God?

Then I gave the answer: because Felix Manalo didn't start off claiming to be a prophet. Originally Iglesia ni Cristo was just another Protestant sect, one that borrowed heavily from the American Campbellites. It wasn't until 1922, when there was a schism within Iglesia ni Cristo, that Manalo started to say he was a prophet. He said that because he wanted the members of his fledgling church to take his side, not the schismatics' side.

Iglesia ni Cristo's anti-Catholicism is not very inventive—that, or the attention span of Iglesia people is remarkably short. *Pasugo* brings up the same charges again and again, yet there's no indication that devoted readers tire of hearing the same thing, even in the same words. Two, three, even four times a year there will be feature stories decrying the same Catholic belief or practice. I don't mean stories that mention a topic briefly and then move on. I mean stories that are almost word-for-word identical.

One of the favorite topics is the identity of the beast of Revelation, the symbolic number of which is 666. Most reputable scholars, Catholic and Protestant, say the number refers to the Roman Emperor Nero. Not all agree, but no such scholars say the beast is the papacy. But that's exactly what Iglesia ni Cristo says. In itself that's not surprising. After all, countless Fundamentalists say the same thing. But Iglesia ni Cristo, in *Pasugo*, says it in a most peculiar way. It makes a bold argument which any attentive reader can disprove simply by glancing at *Pasugo* itself.

The argument goes like this. The number 666 is the sum of the letters of the beast's title. The pope's title is *Vicarius Filii Dei*, Vicar of the Son of God. (Actually, it's not. His title is *Vicarius Christi*, Vicar of Christ). We know this is the papal title because it appears prominently on the tiara of the popes; the letters are formed out of hundreds of jewels. *Vicarius Filii Dei* tallies to 666, which means the papacy is the beast. End of proof.

The editors of *Pasugo* must count on the magazine's readers being inattentive. They print as part of the article a line drawing of the tiara with the words *Vicarius Filii Dei* lettered in, just so you know where they appear. Then—and this shows real chutzpah—they print a photograph of Pope Paul VI, the last pope to wear the tiara. Of course, in the photograph there's no hint of any lettering on the tiara. The photograph contradicts both the text and the line drawing, but no one seemed aware of that until I pointed it out during the debate.

Ventilacion did the only proper thing. He ignored my point and changed the subject. He had a wonderful way of doing this. My favorite example concerns the translation of scriptural passages which supposedly include the name of his sect. This is a major issue with Iglesia members. They believe the Bible mentions their church by name. They desperately want to find the phrase "Church of Christ" in the sacred text.

Their argument is facile: "What is the name of Christ's church, as given in the Bible? It is the 'Church of Christ.' Our church is called the 'Church of Christ.' Therefore, ours is the church Christ founded." Not many people will be impressed with such an argument—when it was first presented to me during a question-and-answer period some years ago, I had trouble not laughing aloud—but the folks at the debate thought it made a lot of sense. The problem was that the verse Ventilacion was citing didn't contain the phrase "Church of Christ." I noted that the Greek means "Church of God," not "Church of Christ." He didn't seem to care.

Of all the debates I've been in, this was at once the most frightening and the most frustrating. It was the most frightening because Iglesia ni Cristo is a true cult, not a mere sect, and it was easy to see why bodyguards were *de rigueur*, even if their muscle wasn't needed this night. And the debate was the most frustrating because my opponent wouldn't adhere to elementary norms of civility and because the audience, at least the Iglesia portion of it, seemed impervious to even the simplest argument against its position. But judge for yourself, as you read the transcript.

Notes on the Text

The following transcript has been edited for clarity and concision. I have taken the liberty of correcting grammatical errors and obvious misstatements, and I have removed those seemingly unavoidable hesitations and starts (ah's and um's and their cousins) that may not be particularly off-putting when spoken but seem to gouge the eyes when in print. The four debates in the series have been made roughly uniform in length. When given publicly, they ranged from two hours to an almost unendurable four hours, counting question-and-answer sessions. Each is now short enough to be read at a single sitting.

I have attempted to retain each speaker's best arguments, feeling no temptation to omit my opponents' most persuasive comments. (I think the Catholic position, however inadequately expressed by me, is match enough for any charge leveled against it.) I have omitted or truncated exchanges that were redundant or seemed unhelpful to the audiences. Also omitted have been audience questions that strayed too far from the topics of the debates or that were not true questions but attempted preaching sessions.

Looking back at my own arguments, particularly those made when on defense, I find places where I could have made a better reply. I have not gussied up my remarks. A reader may say, "But you could have said *this*!" My excuse must be that *this* didn't occur to me at that moment. Perhaps I was taken off guard. Perhaps my mind went blank. Perhaps I just didn't yet know the best answer and could offer only the second-best answer. What is presented here is verisimilitude. I can use a phrase from nineteenth-century German historian Leopold von Ranke. I have attempted to give the story "*wie es eigentlich gewesen*"—"how it really was."

And how it really is today. There is not a single anti-Catholic claim in these books that has fallen out of circulation. The claims have been around for lifetimes, and there is no likelihood that they ever will disappear completely, human nature and human obstinacy being what they are. I have tried to respond to the claims with candor and fairness. Whether I have succeeded is for readers to judge. Throughout the debates I kept in mind that "the truth shall set you free." I always have found searching for truth—and debating what is true—to be exhilarating. I hope you will too, as you read what follows, and I hope these pages bring solace and confidence to Catholics and intrigue and light to non-Catholics.

Debate Transcript
Karl Keating vs. Jose Ventilacion

MODERATOR: Tonight we will discuss, in a debate, two subjects: one is that the holy, catholic, apostolic, and Roman Church is the only true Church, according to the Bible. That's the first proposition. The second proposition will be that the Church of Christ which appeared in the Philippines in 1914 is the only true Church, according to the Bible.

I'd like to emphasized certain rules in this debate. I'm sure that you are all very eager to hear the speakers and that you have your favorite. We do not allow booing, yelling, shouting, stomping your feet, or heckling. In case there is any violence—we don't expect that tonight—arrests will be made. There are policemen here. So I hope that's clear. And now we will start with the debate, and I'd like to bring in Mr. Keating as the first speaker.

KEATING: Thank you, Mr. Moderator. I want to thank Jose Ventilacion for agreeing to this debate. I want to thank all of you for coming.

What is the true Church? That's the question for tonight. I'm not going to leave you in suspense. I'll give you the answer right up front. The true Church, established by Jesus Christ, is the Catholic Church. It is the only one entitled to call itself the Church of Christ.

Let's look at some of the credentials of the Catholic Church. First, historical continuity. It is the only church that can trace itself all the way back to apostolic times. The Eastern Orthodox churches broke off from Rome in 1054. The Protestant churches broke off at the time of the Reformation in the sixteenth century. Iglesia ni Cristo was established in 1914. It has no historical continuity. Only the Catholic Church goes all the way back, and even Iglesia ni Cristo admits that. It acknowledges that in the first century the Catholic Church already was existing.

Another point: apostolic succession. The Catholic Church maintains full apostolic authority. What does that mean? It means today's Catholic bishops are in a direct line from the apostles who received their authority from Jesus Christ himself. In the New Testament, we see our Lord saying to the apostles and consequently to their successors, "Who hears you hears me." No other church can claim this. We see the apostles passing on their authority by laying on of hands, ordaining bishops and priests. In the Book of Acts, we see the first occasion of this when a replacement was obtained for Judas by the laying on of hands. Iglesia ni Cristo entirely lacks this continuity.

Then there is Christ's own promises. Look what he said about the continuity of his Church. Matthew 16:18: "Thou art Peter and upon this rock I will build my Church, and the gates of hell will not prevail against it." Will not prevail against it. Matthew 28:20: "I am with you always, even until the end of the world." Always. John 14:16: "I will pray to the Father and he will give you another comforter who will abide with you forever." Christ promised that nothing would prevail against his Church, that he would be with it always, and that the Holy Spirit, the comforter, the Third Person of the Trinity, would be with it always.

Was Jesus Christ a liar? I suppose Iglesia ni Cristo must say yes because it says Jesus Christ was not with the Church always. The Holy Spirit was not with the Church always. They abandoned the Church in the first century, and it fell into complete apostasy. That's what not being with the true Church implies. If you do say that Jesus Christ is not a liar—and I believe that's what you say—then you must admit that you are not accepting everything that Scripture teaches. The Catholic Church is the only one that maintains the fullness of scriptural doctrine.

We can talk about any number of points. Let me bring out one. Look at

John 6. Do you know what happened in John 6? Jesus had just finished miraculously producing natural food for his followers, from loaves and fishes. Then he said he will give them spiritual food that also will come miraculously. He said, "If there is to be spiritual life within you, you must eat my flesh and drink my blood." What did the Jews who were listening think? They said, "How can this man give us his flesh to eat?" They took him literally. And what did Jesus *not* do? He did not correct them. He did not say, "No, no, you misunderstood me." Remember, whenever he was talking and the crowds didn't get the message, he at least took the apostles aside and said, "Okay, you guys, this is what I mean." He didn't do that this time because nobody misunderstood him when they took him literally. They understood him correctly.

He repeated himself, "Eat my flesh, drink my blood." Then what happened? Some of his disciples, those who had accepted everything up to this point, said, "This is a hard saying. Who can accept it? And they walked with him no more." This is the only place in the New Testament where anybody left Jesus for a doctrinal reason. And you know who also left at that time, did not walk away from him but left him in his heart? Look in verse 64. It was Judas. Judas fell away here because he would not accept the Real Presence of Jesus in the Eucharist. Think about that doctrine. It is a doctrine which the Iglesia ni Cristo refuses to accept. It is one that the Catholic Church always has taught.

Iglesia ni Cristo is known more for its anti-Catholicism than for anything else. Do you read its magazine, *Pasugo*? I've gone through a number of issues. There are many articles in each issue against the Catholic Church but few that are pro-Iglesia ni Cristo. Why this emphasis on the Catholic Church? Because Iglesia ni Cristo agrees with Mormonism. You know in what? In this: Mormons will tell you, if you ask them, that if their church is not the true church, the only other possibility is the Catholic Church. By implication, Iglesia ni Cristo is saying the same thing. If it's not us, it must be you. Only the Catholic Church is the focus of all these barbs.

Have you ever noticed how the attacks on the Catholic Church verge on the fantastic, on the incredible? No serious scholar of any camp could accept them. No serious lay reader could accept them unless he has closed his mind. I'll give you one example that may be brought up later, the nonsensical charge that the pope is the beast of Revelation, whose number is 666. This is one of Iglesia ni Cristo's favorite comments. It appears in its magazine as often as every four issues, but it is nonsense. It has no scriptural warrant, no historical warrant. But why this constant attack against the Catholic Church? Because Iglesia ni Cristo's own doctrines are so weak they could not stand up if given in isolation. There must be a bogeyman out there to go after. The Nazis had the Jews; Iglesia ni Cristo has the Catholic Church.

Let me summarize. The Catholic Church is the only church with complete historical credentials. Iglesia ni Cristo has none. The Catholic Church is the only church that has preserved all the original Christian doctrines. Iglesia ni Cristo ignores or contradicts many of them. The Catholic Church is the only church based solidly on the whole of Scripture, omitting nothing. Iglesia ni Cristo is famous for misapplying Scripture. Iglesia ni Cristo claims to be the Christian Church of the New Testament, but it is not. Iglesia ni Cristo claims to get its distinctive doctrines straight from Scripture, but it does not. Iglesia ni Cristo claims that Felix Manalo was a messenger sent from God, but he was not. Iglesia ni Cristo claims to be the Church of Christ, but it is not. It is only the Catholic Church that has a solid foundation in history, in Scripture, and in reason. Iglesia ni Cristo is neither historical, nor scriptural, nor reasonable as, I am confident, Mr. Ventilacion will now proceed to demonstrate.

VENTILACION: Let me ask you on your basic doctrines, Mr. Keating. You mentioned Matthew 16:18, right.

KEATING: Right.

VENTILACION: Okay. You mentioned about the rock on which a church was built, right?

KEATING: That's right. Peter is the rock.

VENTILACION: Peter is the rock. Thank you. You believe that Peter is the foundation stone of your Church?

KEATING: He is the earthly head of the Church, appointed by Jesus Christ, who himself is the cornerstone of the Church.

VENTILACION: I'm asking you the question: is he the foundation stone of your church? Yes or no, Mr. Keating.

KEATING: I've just answered the question, Mr. Ventilacion.

VENTILACION: Is he a foundation stone?

KEATING: He is a foundation stone because Jesus Christ says so.

VENTILACION: Don't you also teach in your doctrines that Jesus Christ is also a foundation stone?

KEATING: Of course.

VENTILACION: Therefore, in the Catholic Church, you are teaching two kinds of foundation stones.

KEATING: Of course.

VENTILACION: You have two foundation stones?

KEATING: An earthly foundation established by Jesus Christ, and Jesus Christ himself, the ultimate foundation.

VENTILACION: Whether it is an earthly or heavenly foundation, you are teaching two foundation stones, right?

KEATING: Of different qualities and different kinds.

VENTILACION: Thank you. Now, in 1 Corinthians 3:11 of the Good News Bible, which is the Catholic study edition, it says that, "For God has already placed Jesus Christ as the one and only foundation". Do you agree with that?

KEATING: He is the one and only ultimate foundation, of course.

VENTILACION: I am not saying ultimate. The Bible is saying, "For God has already placed Jesus Christ as the one and only foundation." Do you agree with that? That Christ is the only—

KEATING: I've answered that already.

VENTILACION: So you agree?

KEATING: Of course I agree. I agree with the entire Bible. And I noticed you have not said anything about what is the rock in Matthew 16:18. Are you going to ask me about that?

VENTILACION: I'm asking you, please, on what I am presenting so please answer, Mr. Keating.

KEATING: Go right ahead.

VENTILACION: "For God has already placed Jesus Christ as the one and only foundation." Do you agree that Christ is the one and only foundation? Yes or no.

KEATING: That's the third time you've asked the question. Did anybody else miss my answer? I said, three times now, yes, Jesus Christ is the foundation of the Church.

VENTILACION: Now, it says here the one and only foundation. Do you agree with that?

KEATING: I agree with that, if you take it correctly.

VENTILACION: Now, this is the follow-up question.

KEATING: Go ahead.

VENTILACION: The verse also says, Mr. Keating, "And no other foundation can be laid." Do you agree with that?

KEATING: I agree with the whole Bible.

VENTILACION: Okay, now. If Jesus Christ is the one and only foundation, how could you place Peter as another foundation?

KEATING: I can because Jesus Christ said that on Peter he would build his Church.

VENTILACION: If Jesus Christ is the one and only foundation and the Bible says "no other foundation can be laid"—do you accept that?

KEATING: Of course.

VENTILACION: Okay, thank you. So, you believe now that you have laid the apostle Peter as another foundation.

KEATING: I haven't laid Peter as anything. Jesus Christ did.

VENTILACION: Jesus Christ laid the apostle Peter as the foundation stone?

KEATING: Matthew 16:18: "Thou art Peter and upon this rock I will build my Church." The word "rock" refers to Peter.

VENTILACION: Does the word "Peter" means stone or foundation stone?

KEATING: It means foundation stone. Large massive stone. Rock.

VENTILACION: I'm not asking you if he is a rock. I'm asking you if Peter means stone or foundation stone.

KEATING: The new name given to the apostle Simon means large, massive rock as used in a foundation.

VENTILACION: I'm not asking you as if it is a large, massive rock. I'm asking you the meaning of the word. Is Peter the foundation stone or simply a stone?

KEATING: Neither one. Rock. Don't you know the Greek?

VENTILACION: That is not your time to ask questions, Mr. Keating. You will have time to ask questions. You said that Peter is the foundation stone, right? Where could you find a verse in the Bible that says Peter is a foundation stone?

KEATING: I said Peter is the rock.

VENTILACION: Just a stone, not a foundation stone.

KEATING: I said the rock on which the Church would be built. Now—

VENTILACION: Well, that's your own opinion. I'm asking you—

KEATING: That's what Jesus Christ says in Matthew 16:18. It's not my opinion. It's what the verse says.

VENTILACION: That is your opinion. I'm asking you now where does it say in the Bible that Peter is the foundation stone? What verse?

KEATING: Matthew 16:18 says Peter is the rock—

VENTILACION: It doesn't say there that—

MODERATOR: Time is up. We will now hear the negative side of the proposition. Brother Ventilacion.

VENTILACION: We are here not personally against Mr. Keating. We are not against the Catholics. We are not against anybody here. We are not against any Catholic member here. We are against the false teachings of the Roman Catholic Church because the system, or the teachings, that they are presenting to you are not in the Bible.

I went to the basic doctrine of the Catholic Church because the basis of their teaching that theirs is the true Church is because the apostle Peter is the foundation stone upon which Christ built the Church. And because the apostle Peter was the foundation stone, the apostle Peter has successors, the popes, so it means then that because there are popes until this time, so the Catholic Church can trace back its origin from the apostle Peter, who was the first pope. But is that true? Once we have proven today that Peter was not the foundation stone of the Church, built by our Lord Jesus Christ, then the reasoning of Mr. Keating that theirs is the true Church will crumble.

According to Matthew 16:18, who is the rock or the foundation stone upon which the Church was built? Let us examine chapter 16:18. It says here, "And so I tell you, Peter, you are a rock and on this rock foundation I will build my Church. And that evil will never be able to overcome it." Christ is the one speaking. He did not say to Peter. "You are a rock foundation." He said here, "And I tell you, you are rock, and on this rock foundation, I will build my Church." That's why I asked him, "Is Peter the foundation stone?" He said, "Yes." In the Catholic Bible, which is the Douay-Rheims version, they also state that Jesus Christ is the chief foundation stone. What I am holding now is the Douay-Rheims version, which is the Catholic version. It says here in the footnote, "Christ himself, the chief foundation stone." Now, if Peter is the foundation stone and Christ is also the foundation stone, then it means then that they have two foundation stones.

According to 1 Corinthians 3:11, could you put another foundation? That's what the Catholic Church did. In 1 Corinthians 3:11, it says here, "For God has already placed Jesus Christ as the one and only foundation, and no other foundation can be laid." When they place the apostle Peter as another foundation, they are violating the Scriptures. The Bible says, "No other foundation can be laid." That's why I asked him, if Jesus Christ is the one and only foundation, could Peter be a foundation? He said, "Yes."

That answer, Mr. Keating, is going against the teaching of the Bible that you could not lay or place any other foundation aside from what God has placed. And you could not read, from the Bible, that God placed the apostle Peter as the foundation of the Church. What you can read, Mr. Keating, is that God has already placed Jesus Christ as the one and only foundation. So what happens now to the claims of the Catholic Church, that theirs is the true Church because Christ built his Church upon Peter? That claim is not in the Bible. It is a misunderstanding of the meaning of Christ's statement in Matthew 16:18.

Let us ask the apostle Peter, according to the apostle Peter, who is the stone which was rejected, which became the cornerstone? Did he introduce himself as the foundation stone? Let us ask the apostle Peter in Acts 4:10–11: "Be it known to you all and to all the people of Israel that by the name of our Lord Jesus Christ of Nazareth, this is the stone which was rejected by you the builders which has become the head of the corner." What did the apostle Peter say? He did not say, "I am the stone." He said, "This is the stone," referring to our Lord Jesus Christ. I would like Mr. Karl Keating to show us proof, from the Bible, that the apostle Peter teaches himself as the foundation stone. Even in his letter, in the letter of the apostle Peter to the Christians, whom did he preach or teach as the foundation stone?

He said this in 1 Peter 2:5–6: "Be you also as the living stones built up, a spiritual house, a holy priesthood to offer up spiritual sacrifices acceptable to

God by Jesus Christ." What did the Bible say? The apostle Peter himself said even in his letter—he was pointing to our Lord Jesus Christ as the foundation of the Church. Remember that this letter was addressed to the Church. He said to them, "You are also living stones built up as spiritual house." They know that spiritual house is the Church. And the apostle Peter is teaching them that the stone in which the spiritual house was built is Christ Jesus.

That's why I challenge Mr. Keating to show a verse in the Bible that Peter said, "I am the foundation stone." Nobody could read that. What you can read from the Bible is that the apostle Peter mentioned that Christ is the foundation stone. Well there could be a secondary stone, that's what they are saying, because Christ is the chief foundation stone and Peter is the secondary stone. But, again, let me rephrase—let me, again, mention 1 Corinthians 3:11: "No other foundation can be laid."

What did the apostle Peter say concerning the stone that was placed by God? What would other people do with the stone? I'll read again the statement of the apostle Peter here in Acts 4:10–11: "Be it known to ye all and to all the people of Israel that by the name of our Lord Jesus Christ of Nazareth, this is the stone which was rejected by you the builders, which is to become the head of the corner." What did the apostle Peter say the people shall do concerning the stone, the foundation stone of the Church? He said, "They will reject it." That's why the Catholic Church replaced Jesus Christ. They said when Jesus Christ went up to heaven, he was replaced by the apostle Peter. It's like Jesus Christ, according to them, is the invisible head of the Church, and the apostle Peter is the head of the Church.

Now, let's continue. In Ephesians 2:20, here is another apostle. What did the apostle Paul say about the foundation of the Church? Did he say, "Well, my fellow apostle Peter is the foundation stone"? What did he say? He said, "Build upon the foundation of the apostles and prophets, Jesus Christ himself being the chief cornerstone in whom all the building being framed together groweth up into a holy temple in the Lord." According to the apostle Paul, who is the foundation stone? He said, "Jesus Christ himself." He said, "Built upon the foundation of the apostles and the prophets." Because the apostles and the prophets were in the Church, they too were built upon Christ. Is the apostle Peter an apostle? Yes. Is he built upon Christ? Yes.

If Peter is a foundation stone and he is built upon Jesus Christ, what shall appear, my beloved friends? Then it appears that the foundation stone is built upon another foundation stone. And that is not in the Bible. The Bible never mentioned a foundation stone that is built upon another foundation stone. But that is what is appearing if we shall follow the line of reasoning of the Roman Catholic Church. Now, Mr. Keating, instead of resorting to proving that their church is the true Church from the Bible, I was watching him. If he was opening the Bible, he did not. He was just merely quoting the Bible.

The resolution states, "Resolved, that the Catholic Church is the only true Church, according to the Bible." Where did he go? Apostolicity, and he mentioned other things. Why don't you read the Bible to show that the Catholic Church is indeed the true Church, why don't you read the Bible? You could not read from the Bible the words "Catholic Church." Why? Because that name was only invented by St. Ignatius of Antioch. That's why we should not be surprised, my beloved friends, that Mr. Keating is not even opening the Bible to prove his contention that the Catholic Church is indeed the true Church.

Now, why don't we examine their teachings? I believe that there are a lot of Catholic friends here who give honor to Mary. The Catholic Church claims that they are united, not only in government but even in doctrines or teachings. That's what they claim. That's why the four marks for the Catholic Church, they said, are one, holy, catholic, and apostolic. Let us go to the so-called unity. Are they united in their doctrines?

MODERATOR: Thank you Brother Ventilacion. We will have a seven-minute rebuttal from Mr. Keating.

VENTILACION: He will first question me for five minutes.

MODERATOR: Oh is that what it is?

KEATING: I'd like to point out to you that the debate is not being conducted on the terms that Mr. Ventilacion and I agreed to in writing. You'll notice, it's three against one. It's unbalanced.

VENTILACION: Don't mislead the audience. You said a while ago, "It's okay Jose that you have the two seconds. Why are you trying to point this out to the audience?

KEATING: When I came up to him before the debate and complained about him having helpers, he said, "If you don't agree to this we'll cancel the debate." I know many of you drove a long way. I'm not going to do that to you. So, let me ask a question now. Let's get—

VENTILACION: Why don't we ask the moderator here, because he knows what transpired before this debate.

KEATING: No, that is when you and I talked privately. He was not here yet.

VENTILACION: Why don't you ask the moderator, and ask him if you agreed that I have two seconds here during this debate. Did you agree or not?

KEATING: After you threatened to quit, yes. What was I going to do, disappoint everybody?

VENTILACION: I said, I'm not quitting. I said we will not do this debate if you will not agree that I have these two people here. Did I say I quit?

KEATING: If you say, "If you don't give me your money, I'll shoot you," of course I'll give you my money. Now to my question. Let's get back to Matthew 16:18. You were skirting around it. Jesus says to Peter, "You are Peter and upon this rock I will build my Church." Who is the rock?

VENTILACION: The rock is Christ.

KEATING: What makes you say the rock is Christ?

VENTILACION: Matthew 16:18, Catholic version, mentions that Christ himself is the true foundation stone.

KEATING: You are avoiding my question.

VENTILACION: I'm not avoiding your question.

KEATING: In Matthew 16:18, let's get to the meaning of the word. What language did Jesus speak?

VENTILACION: He spoke in Aramaic. That's what you were telling the people?

KEATING: That's correct. He was speaking in Aramaic.

VENTILACION: It was translated to Greek.

KEATING: That's right. Now, what name in Aramaic did Peter get? What is "Peter" in Aramaic?

VENTILACION: *Kepha.* That is what you said in your book.

KEATING: *Kepha.* That's right. You read my book.

VENTILACION: *Kepha,* which means a stone. Not a foundation stone.

KEATING: You said you read my book. You should know better. [Speaking to one of Mr. Ventilacion's seconds.] Why don't you get him my book and bring it up? The word "*Kepha*" in Aramaic means exactly the same as the Greek word "*Petra,*" large rock.

VENTILACION: This is my answer Mr. Keating. My answer is this. The apostle Peter was the direct audience of our Lord Jesus Christ. When he said that Christ is the stone, upon which the Church was built, I agree with the apostle Peter. Don't you agree with him?

KEATING: Again, I am asking the questions.

VENTILACION: Okay.

KEATING: You still didn't answer my question. Apparently, you admit that Peter's name, in Aramaic, is *Kepha*?

VENTILACION: Yes, we do not deny that, Mr. Keating.

KEATING: And you admit that the word "*Kepha*" means either a stone or rock? Which one?

VENTILACION: Yes, I agree with that. But it is not Peter who is the foundation stone.

KEATING: Which one? Is it stone or rock? They're different things.

VENTILACION: It's the same, Mr. Keating.

KEATING: Greek has different words for it. English has different words for it. Aramaic has different words. In Aramaic, the word for stone is "*ephna*."

VENTILACION: What is your question, now?

KEATING: I want you to answer the same one. Are you saying that in Aramaic the word "*kepha*" means a mere stone?

VENTILACION: In John 1, the apostle Peter was named. This is from John

1:42. Jesus looked at him and said, "Your name is Simon, son of John, but you will be called Cephas." This is the same as Peter and means a rock.

KEATING: That's right. Thank you. It means rock. So, "Thou art Peter—Rock—and upon this rock." That's what I was driving at. Now I have a different question. You said, as a conclusive argument against the Catholic Church, the name "Catholic Church" does not appear in Scripture. True. Where does the name "Church of Christ" or "Iglesia ni Cristo" appear?

VENTILACION: I'm going to read for Mr. Keating. Acts 20:28.

KEATING: Acts 20:28? That's what I was waiting for.

VENTILACION: Aramaic, the language of Jesus, Mr. Keating. From the Aramaic, "Take ye therefore to yourselves and to all the flock over which the Holy Spirit has appointed you overseers to feed the church of Christ." Translated from the Aramaic—translated from the Aramaic, the language of Jesus. Thank you.

KEATING: That was the Lamsa version, I presume?

VENTILACION: This is the Lamsa version, translated from the Aramaic, the language of Jesus. You follow that Aramaic.

KEATING: The version that we all accept, the official version, is in Greek. The word in Greek, there in that passage, Acts 20:28, is "churches," not singular "church."

[Talking over one another.]

VENTILACION: Your question is could you find the Church of Christ in the Bible. I read it. So what? What's next?

MODERATOR: It's getting more interesting, isn't it? Now we will have a seven-minute rebuttal from Mr. Keating.

KEATING: Now that I have the floor to myself, I want to point out something: in Greek, it is not "church of Christ," it is "churches of Christ." The phrase "Church of Christ" as such, the phrase "Catholic Church" as such—neither one appears in the New Testament. Saying that the word or phrase doesn't appear means nothing. I don't argue against the Iglesia ni Cristo because its name isn't in the Bible. That's a dumb way to argue, and I don't think Mr. Ventilacion ought to argue against the Catholic Church because its formal name is not there either. That proves nothing.

Let's go to another issue. One of the constant teachings of the Catholic Church is the divinity of Jesus Christ. This is a doctrine that Iglesia ni Cristo opposes. It says that Jesus Christ is not God but a creature, maybe the highest creature but still a creature. The ancient name for that heresy was Arianism.

Let's look at what the Bible says. John 1:1. Open your Bibles if you have them. "In the beginning was the Word and the Word was with God, and the Word was God." Now, who was the Word? We find the answer in John 1:14: "And the Word was made flesh and dwelt among us." Was it God the Father who was made flesh? No. Jesus Christ was made flesh and dwelt among us. The Son of God. Therefore, he is the Word, and in John 1:1, the Word is called divine. He's called God. Iglesia ni Cristo takes the Jehovah Witnesses' position here.

In 1 Timothy 6:15, God is also called "the blessed and only potentate, the King of Kings and Lord of Lords." What about Jesus Christ? He's called the same thing. Revelation 17:14: "They shall make war with the lamb"—the lamb is Jesus Christ—"and the lamb shall overcome them, for he is Lord of Lords and King of Kings." Jesus Christ, then, is God.

Look at Revelation 19:16, which is referring to the word of God: "On his thigh a name is written, King of Kings, Lord of Lords"—the same titles that define God the Father define Jesus Christ. God the Father is called the first and the last. Isaiah 44:6: "I am the first, and I am the last." Jesus is also the first and the last. Revelation 22:13: "I am the Alpha and the Omega, the beginning and the end, the first and the last." And Revelation 1:17: "I am the first and the last, I am he that liveth and was dead who rose from the dead." Who is that? Jesus Christ, the first and the last. The Father did not die and rise again. Jesus gives himself the same proper name that God the Father has. God calls himself "I Am" in Exodus 3:14. "Thus thou shalt say unto the children of Israel, I Am has sent me unto you." And Jesus says in John 8:58, "Before Abraham was, I Am"—not "I was" but "I Am."

Look at some other verses. In Colossians 2:9, Paul tells us, "In Christ the fullness of deity dwells bodily." Isaiah 45:23 says, "To God every knee shall bow." In Philippians 2:10 Paul says that to Christ "every knee shall bow." Christ gets the same worship as God the Father. Remember, if you read *Pasugo*, that Iglesia ni Cristo says, "If you bow down to something or somebody, you are worshiping it or him, and you only worship God." The Bible says you should bow down to Jesus. So, the Bible says you're to worship him, which means he must be God.

Lastly, let's look at John 21:28: "And Thomas answered and said unto him, 'My Lord and my God.'" What does Iglesia ni Cristo say? "Oh, Thomas was just mistaken." But Jesus does not correct Thomas. He accepts his acknowledgement of his lordship, his divinity.

MODERATOR: Thank you, Mr. Keating. We now have a three-minute cross question by Brother Ventilacion.

VENTILACION: Mr. Keating, I have the book which is entitled *Religion: Doctrine and Practice,* which is written by your priest. It says here that Jesus Christ established the Church. Yes, from all history books, secular and profane, as well as from the Bible, considered as a human document, we learn that Jesus Christ established the Church, which from the earliest times is being called after him, the Christian Church or the Church of Christ. Do you agree with this?

KEATING: The Church that Jesus Christ established, obviously, has been called the Church of Christ.

VENTILACION: Your priest said it's from the Bible. What verse is that in the Bible that Christ—

KEATING: I don't know who you are quoting.

VENTILACION: This is Francis Cassilly.

KEATING: I have no idea who he is.

VENTILACION: You don't know who he is?

KEATING: No. And the book looks about 60 years old.

VENTILACION: He is from Creighton University in Omaha, Nebraska. This is from the Society of Jesus. This is an imprimatur of George Cardinal Mundelein. My question is: do you agree with Mr. Cassilly that the Church was called the Church of Christ since the earliest of times?

KEATING: That's correct, but it's not in the Bible.

VENTILACION: Do you also agree that the Bible says that it is the Church of Christ?

KEATING: It does not use the phrase "Church of Christ." That does not mean it is not the Church of Christ. It is the Church of Christ but that phrase happens not to be used.

VENTILACION: Is this here, as it's been called after him, the Christian Church or the Church of Christ? It was called the Church of Christ. It's from the Bible. What Bible does it say that the Church of Christ is the church established by Christ?

KEATING: I don't understand that question. Try it again.

VENTILACION: Okay. I repeat. Your priest said that Christ established the Church of Christ, quoting the Bible. What verse says that Christ established the Church of Christ?

KEATING: It says that he would establish his own Church in Matthew 16:18. We can take him at his word that he established it.

VENTILACION: I'm asking about the words "Church of Christ." Where did you find that in the Bible?

KEATING: I explained earlier that it's not in the Bible.

VENTILACION: It's not in the Bible?

KEATING: Not the singular, no.

VENTILACION: But your priest said it is from the Bible.

KEATING: Does he give a citation?

VENTILACION: Okay, never mind. Next question. Peter is the first pope, right?

KEATING: That's right.

VENTILACION: During the Council of Jerusalem—which you call the Council of Jerusalem; I call it the meeting of the apostles—during that time, in the Council of Jerusalem, Peter was pope, already?

KEATING: That's right.

VENTILACION: Okay. Now, during the time that they should have a decision, concerning the Gentiles who were turning to God, who made the judgment or decision? Was it the apostle Peter or the apostle James?

KEATING: Although James spoke last, he agreed with Peter's decision which was spoken earlier.

VENTILACION: I'm asking you who made the decision? Is it Peter or James?

KEATING: Peter.

VENTILACION: Peter? What verse, in the same chapter, do you find that the apostle Peter said, "This is my decision." What verse in chapter 15?

KEATING: He didn't use those words, and neither did James.

VENTILACION: If I could read from the Bible that the apostle James said, "This is my judgment or decision," would you accept then that apostle James is the leader of the Church during the apostolic times?

KEATING: Of course not.

VENTILACION: You will not? Okay. Therefore, I will read.

MODERATOR: Sorry, gentlemen. We now go to a 7-minute rebuttal by Brother Ventilacion.

VENTILACION: Mr. Keating could not prove that his church is the true Church, so he went to proving that Christ is God. Well we could have a debate concerning Christ or the Trinity if he would like, but that's not the point of our debate here, Mr. Keating. The point of our debate is to prove which church is the true Church. If you could not prove that your church is the true Church, how much then could you prove that Christ is God? I'll be waiting if you would like to challenge this.

I'm going to read again from this book. Mr. Keating is not familiar with this book. It is by Francis Cassilly, a member of the Society of Jesus, one of the learned priests, according to their standard. He said that Christ established the Church since the earliest times. Where did the priest learn that Christ established the Church since the earliest times? He said from history as well as from the Bible. What was the name of the Church that was established by Christ? The priest also said that it was called after Christ, the Church of Christ—of course, because it was Christ who built the Church. He could not call it the Catholic Church. It was not Catholic who established the church. That name, "Catholic," came from St. Ignatius of Antioch, and it is outside of the Bible.

Now, let's continue. I will not go to whether Jesus Christ is God or not. We will go to the basic doctrines of the Catholic Church. They said that the apostle Peter was the first pope during the Council of Jerusalem. Now, let's find out if that is true. Who made the decision that they should no longer trouble the Gentiles? He said the apostle Peter made the decision. I asked him, what if I could read that it was apostle James who made the decision? Now, let's find out. What did the apostle Peter say?

This is in Acts 15:7: "After much discussion, Peter took the floor and said to them, 'Brothers, you know well that from the early days God selected me from your number to be one from whose lips the Gentiles would hear the message of the gospel and believe. God, who reads the hearts of men, showed his approval by granting the Holy Spirit to them, just as he did to us. He made no distinction between them and us that purify their hearts by means of faith also. Why, then, do you put God to the test by trying to place on the shoulders of this convert a yoke which neither we nor our fathers were able to bear?"

He never said "This is my decision." He never said "This is my judgment." Who else spoke after the apostle Peter that the whole assembly fell silent? They listened to Barnabas and Paul. When they had concluded the presentation, James spoke up. "Brothers," he said, "listen to me." He told the apostles, "Listen to me," including the apostle Peter. He said, "It is my judgment, therefore, that we ought not to cause God's Gentile converts any difficulties." Well, what I am reading is the Holy Bible, the New American Bible, the new Catholic translation.

Now, if the apostle Peter was the first pope, would it not be, Mr. Keating, a usurpation of the authority of the apostle Peter? Look at that, a pope in person at a council and somebody subordinate would make a decision for him? That's why the apostle Peter is not the first pope. Therefore, their foundation is crumbling again. It is crumbling again. It was not the apostle Peter who made a decision. That's in the Bible. I challenge him again. Show a verse in the Bible that says the apostle Peter said, at the Council of Jerusalem, "This is my judgment" or "This is my decision." Mr. Keating could read a whole chapter of Acts, but he could not find a verse where the apostle Peter would say, "This is my judgment." Rather, it was apostle James who made the decision.

What is the proof, then, that the apostle Peter recognized the authority of the apostle James? When the apostle Peter was released from prison, whom did he tell the members of the Church to tell concerning his release from prison? He motioned to them to be quiet and explained how the Lord had brought him out of prison. Report this to James and the brothers, he told the members of the Church. Report it to James. If Peter was a pope, why then would he tell the members to report it to James? This is the proof that he is not the leader of the Church. In Acts 8:14, it says, "When the apostles in Jerusalem heard that Samaria had accepted the word of God, they sent Peter and John to them." The apostles in Jerusalem sent Peter. How could he be a pope or a leader of the Church when he was sent? Who is greatest, the one that is sent or the one that is sending?

MODERATOR: We now have a three-minute cross-question from Mr. Keating.

KEATING: Mr. Ventilacion, can we tell which is the true Church by its teachings?

VENTILACION: Exactly. That is my position.

KEATING: All right. If Iglesia ni Cristo teaches a false doctrine, would that imply that Iglesia ni Cristo is not the true Church?

VENTILACION: If it is teaching a false doctrine—

KEATING: Yes or no, please.

VENTILACION: I'm answering you.

KEATING: Yes or no.

VENTILACION: If you could find a false doctrine of the Church of Christ, then, this is not the true Church, but I guarantee you, you could not find one.

KEATING: If the Catholic Church, though, teaches true doctrine, you would admit it would have to be the true Church?

VENTILACION: Well, I just presented in my first presentation that you are contradicting yourself concerning your doctrine about the Virgin Mary.

KEATING: Okay. So far you've admitted that the church that teaches truly is true. The one that teaches falsely is false.

VENTILACION: It is. As long as it is the doctrine in the Bible, that is a true doctrine.

KEATING: If Christ really is divine, then Iglesia ni Cristo must not be the true Church. Right?

VENTILACION: Do we believe—

KEATING: I'm not asking you if you believe it. I know what your position is.

VENTILACION: Why don't we have another debate, Mr. Karl Keating, on the deity of Jesus Christ?

KEATING: Because the true Church is identified by its teachings.

VENTILACION: That is not the topic of our debate here.

KEATING: It's exactly the topic. It's exactly the topic of our debate. What I want to get out of you is this: is Jesus Christ—

VENTILACION: Jesus Christ is divine but not God, because even the Christians are partakers of the divine nature. Are we God too?

KEATING: Let me ask you a question maybe you'll answer. In the House of Representatives when the Speaker and the majority leader and the minority leader and the whips are sent by the members of the House to go see the President in the White House, they are sent by the members of the House. Does that imply that the members of the House are above their superiors?

VENTILACION: What you are talking about is not in the Bible.

KEATING: I am asking you a question. You will do anything, won't you, to avoid answering a simple question?

VENTILACION: No, I'm not avoiding.

KEATING: Your point about Peter being sent is that therefore he must be inferior. I've asked you what about the case of the House of Representatives? You're not willing to answer that because you know what the answer would imply.

MODERATOR: Thank you very much, gentlemen. And I'd like to thank the audience, too, for their fine and very peaceful, I would say, demeanor. Now, we're going to end the first portion of the debate.

VENTILACION: When the Church apostatized, then there was a need for Christ to re-establish his Church because the Church is necessary for salvation. Now, according to Dr. Henry Halley, one of the famous biblical authors, he mentioned that the Church had changed its nature, had entered its great apostasy, had become a political organization in the spirit and pattern of Imperial Rome. The proof that there was an apostasy is the Catholic Church itself. We are going to present to you today from the Bible that after the first century the Church was apostatized.

Christ mentioned or prophesied about the re-establishment of his Church. What is the proof, my beloved friends? I'm going to read from John 10:16. Christ mentioned, "Other sheep I have which are not of this fold. They also I must bring, and they will hear my voice, and there will be one flock and one shepherd." In this verse that I am reading, Christ is prophesying about the re-establishment of his Church. Why? Because he said, "I have other sheep, which are not of this fold." What did Christ say that he will do to these other sheep? He said, "I will also bring them, they will hear my voice, and there will be one flock."

What is the meaning of the word "flock"? The flock, according to Acts 20:28, in the Lamsa version of the Bible, which I read a while ago but I have to repeat again: "Take ye therefore to yourselves and to all the flock, over which the Holy Spirit has appointed you overseers, to feed the church of Christ." So, the flock is the Church of Christ. Christ mentioned his other sheep, which will become one flock or one Church of Christ. And this is in the future, because Christ said, "There will be one flock."

So, aside from the flock, during the times of Christ and the apostles, there will still be another flock. Christ said, "My other sheep, they are not of this fold." Why? Where are the other sheep of Christ? Why, suddenly, do they not belong to the first century Church of Christ? Because in Acts 2:39 it says, "For the promises onto you and to your children and to all who are afar off, as many as the Lord our God will call." Why is it that they do not belong to the flock, or to the first century Church? Because God shall call them. They are not yet called to the Church. That is why it is the future. There will be a re-establishment of one Church. Christ said, "My other sheep will become one flock of the Church of Christ." Now, who were called? The apostle Peter said, "They shall be called, or God will call them." Who were called, already, during the time of Christ and the apostles? These are the members of the first-century Church of Christ. Romans 9:24 says, "Even us whom he called, not of the Jews only, but also of the Gentiles." So now, Acts 2:39, when the apostle Peter said, "for the promises to you," he was talking to the Jews, "and to your children" was referring to the Gentiles and to all who are afar off.

These are not Jews or Gentiles. They are the other sheep of Christ. "But God will call them, or God shall bring them." From where? The Bible says, "from afar off." Where is this afar off? Where will the other sheep come from? God himself will answer that question. In Isaiah 43:5 this is what is recorded: "From the far east will I bring your offspring, and from the far west I will gather you." So, what is this far off, where the other sheep of Christ, the third group of people that will constitute the one true church of Christ, will come from? God himself said in the prophecy, "From the far east will I bring your offspring." What country is the fulfillment of this? The Philippines. Why?

The Philippines, no one could deny it, is in the Far East. It is not only in the Far East, a priest by the name of Horacio de la Costa wrote a book entitled *Asia and the Philippines*. On page 169 he said, "It cannot be without significance that the country which stands almost at the geographical center of the Far East, the Philippines, should also be that in which Christianity has taken the deepest root." So, the Philippines is not only in the Far East, it is lying almost at the geographical center of the Far East. So, when Christ said, "I have other sheep," this is the Church of Christ that appeared in the Far East. The country is the Philippines.

According to the same prophecy, when shall God bring this Church of Christ from the Philippines? I read Isaiah 43:5-6 in the King James version: "Fear not for I am with thee. I will bring thy seed from the East and gather thee from the West. I will say to the North and to the South, keep not back. Bring my sons from far and my daughters from the ends of the Earth." Our question is when shall God bring these people from the Far East? God said, "Bring my sons from far and my daughters from the ends of the Earth." That is the time element involved in the prophecy. When you say the ends of the Earth, that is not the same as the end of the Earth or the end of the world. We have to first find out when is the end of the world or end of the Earth.

Matthew 24:3: "And as he sat upon the Mount of Olives, the disciples came unto him privately saying, Tell us when shall these things be? What shall be the sign of thy coming and of the end of the world?" The apostles were asking our Lord Jesus Christ, "When is the end of the world?" They were asking him, "What shall be the sign of thy coming and of the end of the world? When shall these things be?"

The end of the world refers to the Second Coming of Christ. But it is not the time that the Church of Christ will be re-established in the Far East or in the Philippines. God said, in the prophecy, "And the ends of the Earth." When is this? Here is the statement of Christ in Matthew 24:33: "So, likewise, you, when you shall see all these things, know that it is near, even at the doors." What is the first sign, given by Christ? In the same chapter, in Matthew 24:6, he said, "And you shall hear of wars and rumors of wars. See that you be not troubled for all these things must come to pass, but the end is not yet." So, what was the first sign given by our Lord Jesus Christ? He said, "You shall hear of wars and rumors of wars." What war is the fulfillment of this prophecy of our Lord Jesus Christ?

What I am going to read is an excerpt from a book entitled *The Story of the Great War*: "The first campaign of the southeastern battlegrounds of the Great War began on July 27, 1914, when the Austrian troops undertook their first invasion of Serbia." This was a book that was copyrighted 1916, two years after the start of the Great War. They called it the Great War, but historians later called it the First World War. Another book that says the First World War started on July 27, 1914, is *The Nations at War* by Willis J. Abbott. Austria, backed by Germany, declared war upon Serbia on July 27, so the First World War started on July 27, 1914. That is the war mentioned by Christ in Matthew 24:6, "That you shall hear the rumors of wars."

At the same time that we could see the war, we could see the Church of Christ reappeared or re-established in the Philippines. What I have here is a copy of the incorporation record. "This is to certify a copy of the articles of incorporation of Iglesia ni Cristo, dated July 24, 1914, registered on July 27, 1914." The Church of Christ appeared at the same time that the First World War erupted in Europe. Why? Probably our friend here would say, "That is just a matter of coincidence." We do not call it a matter of coincidence because it is a divine mandate. It is in the Bible. God used the phrase "ends of the Earth." The war started on July 27, 1914, at the same time that the Church was registered with the Philippine government as a religious organization.

So, I have proven my point here, my beloved friends, that this Church is, indeed, the Church established by Christ. They would say it is the church established by Manalo. We do not have that kind of doctrine. Ask the members of the Church of Christ that are here now. Ask them, "Who established your church?" If they would say Manalo, then that is wrong. Probably you are asking a Catholic, not an Iglesia ni Cristo. If you will be asking an Iglesia ni Cristo, he would tell you, "It is Jesus Christ, based upon his prophecy in John 10:16 about his other sheep."

Did you hear Mr. Keating say that they deny the deity of Jesus Christ? Why? Because Jesus Christ is not the Father. And our mission here, the mission of the whole Church of Christ now, is to proclaim to the people of the world that there is only one God and that is the Father. He said, three Persons in one God. He could not read. He could not read it from the Bible that God said "I am three Persons." He could not read from the Bible that Christ would say "I am God" or "I am a true God." I guarantee you that. Mr. Keating could not read from the Bible that Jesus Christ himself said, "I am God."

MODERATOR: We now have a five-minute cross-question from the negative side. Mr. Keating.

KEATING: Tell me, where does the Bible use the word "Philippines"?

VENTILACION: Mr. Keating, the word "Philippines" came long after the Bible was written.

KEATING: That's right. It's not in the Bible. Second question.

VENTILACION: The proper word is Far East.

KEATING: Second question. The words "far" and "east" do not appear in the Hebrew in the same sentence.

VENTILACION: It doesn't appear in the same sentence?

KEATING: No. The phrase does not, but I'm going to allow "Far East" for the purposes of argument. Why do you say that Far East must apply to the Philippines, when the Far East includes China, Korea, Japan, Taiwan, Hong Kong, and Indochina?

VENTILACION: Okay. This is it. The whole Far East is not only the Philippines, but the Far East, in Isaiah 43:5, is the Philippines because the Church appeared in the Philippines.

KEATING: You quoted somebody who said that the geographical center of the Far East was the Philippines.

VENTILACION: Center of the Far East.

KEATING: That's right. Has anybody here ever looked at a map of the Far East? Has anybody here ever looked at a world map? If you look at a map of the Far East, the Philippines is in the southeast corner. Please explain how the southeast corner can be the geographic center.

VENTILACION: It's the priest himself.

KEATING: What the priest said doesn't mean anything. The priest is incorrect. You're relying on a priest who happens to know no geography.

VENTILACION: The priest doesn't mean anything, Mr. Keating?

KEATING: His comment means nothing because he happens to be geographically wrong. Is it your opinion that the Philippines is the geographic center of the Far East? I'm asking you, Mr. Ventilacion, if you would dare to say such a foolish thing to a geography teacher?

VENTILACION: Well I'm not, but I'm teaching you—

KEATING: Let me go on to one of your verses. Let's go to Isaiah 43, where it says, "The sons came from far and the daughters from the ends of the Earth." What you did not mention is what the Hebrew original actually says. The Hebrew means "the end" in the sense of space, not of time. It does not use the sense of time.

VENTILACION: That is your opinion.

KEATING: It is not my opinion, it's Hebrew. It's the Hebrew language.

VENTILACION: That's your Hebrew opinion.

KEATING: The Old Testament was written in Hebrew. Do you think it was written in English?

VENTILACION: What I'm talking about is your Hebrew opinion.

KEATING: You are refusing to look at the Hebrew?

VENTILACION: Yes.

KEATING: Yes? Why do you refuse to look at the Hebrew original? Why, because it's against what you believe, right?

VENTILACION: Is it the original Hebrew? Is it not that the original Hebrew was destroyed?

KEATING: We have the Old Testament in Hebrew, do we not? Is it in Hebrew or is it in English?

VENTILACION: You are mentioning Isaiah 43:5, right?

KEATING: Yes. You quoted it in the English. You said the word "ends" refers to time. It does not refer to time. It refers only to space.

MODERATOR: Thank you gentlemen. We now go to a 15-minute talk by the negative side, Mr. Keating.

KEATING: Let me not put too fine a point on it. Iglesia ni Cristo relies for its credentials on a fraudulent history. It claims that the Church that Jesus Christ established entirely apostatized—that is, ceased to exist—in the first century. In my first remarks, I quoted from Matthew 16 where Jesus said he never would abandon the Church. But if the Church ceased to exist because it had no members, that's exactly what he allowed to happen, and so he must have been a liar.

Mr. Ventilacion says, "Oh, the church was restored in 1914." Where have we heard that before? I'll tell you where we've heard it before, and I'll tell you where Felix Manalo got it. In 1830 God supposedly told Joseph Smith to restore the true Church, the Mormon Church. In 1879, God supposedly told Charles Taze Russell, who frequently is cited in *Pasugo* as an authority, to re-establish the true Church. Members of his church are known as Jehovah's Witnesses. In 1879 God supposedly told Mary Baker Eddy to organize the true Church. Hers is known as the Christian Science Church. In 1931 God supposedly told Herbert W. Armstrong that he would be the new messenger who would rise up to found the new Church. He called his church he Worldwide Church of God. In 1936 God supposedly told Sun Yung Moon that he would be the new messenger. This messenger, Moon said, would rise out of the Far East, which is not the Philippines but Korea. Moon's one true Church is called the Unification Church. His followers often are called "Moonies."

Like all these other churches, Iglesia ni Cristo claims that its founder, Felix Manalo, is the true messenger. This is nonsense. Look at the man's background. Although he was baptized a Catholic, he left the Catholic Church as a young teenager. He became a Protestant. He went through five Protestant denominations, including the Seventh-day Adventist Church. Finally, he decided to start his own church, which he did in 1914, but he did not begin with all of today's Iglesia ni Cristo doctrines in place. Maybe you are not told that. In 1919 Manalo went to America because he wanted to learn more about religion. Where did he go? He went to study with Protestants, who, later on, the Iglesia people would say are apostates just like Catholics.

Why, five years after being called by God as the new messenger, did Manalo go to the U.S. to learn from apostates? The fact is that he didn't use the new messenger doctrine in 1914. He didn't use it even in 1919. He didn't use it until 1922. Why? Because there was a schism in Iglesia ni Cristo. Manalo wanted to accumulate as much power as possible, so he raised himself in the eyes of his followers by claiming to be the new messenger. This is balderdash. If he had been the new messenger when called by God in 1914, why didn't he tell anybody until 1922? The answer is because he didn't even know about it until 1922. And he didn't know about it until he learned from the American Seventh-day Adventists and learned from the American Jehovah's Witnesses. He borrowed the distinctive doctrines for his church from American sectarian groups. The lack of divinity for Christ, the lack of the Trinity? That's from the Jehovah's Witnesses. The apostasy of the early Church? That's from the Mormons. You need to find out where your beliefs really come from.

What about World War I and 1914 being the year? Is it just a coincidence that Manalo filed the articles of incorporation for his church, registered it in the Philippines, in 1914? Mr. Ventilacion would have you think, no. He would have you think it was a divine act. He would have you think that World War I was foretold in Isaiah 34:2. Have you ever read Isaiah 34:2 carefully? Read what it says. It says, "All nations and their armies will be involved in the war." That quotation I take from *Pasugo*. That's its understanding of Isaiah 34:2. "All nations of the world."

Did World War I involve all nations, even though it was called a world war? It didn't involve any nations, except for the U.S. and a couple of token troops from elsewhere, from the Western hemisphere. Except for countries like Tanganyika, it didn't include any nations in Africa. Aside from Palestine and Turkey, it didn't include any nations in Asia. It didn't include Australia. It didn't even include all the nations of Europe. Most of the nations of the world did not participate at all in World War I. Don't let yourself be fooled that just because it's called a world war that therefore all the world was involved. That's not the case. If you know any international history, you know that's not the case. So, World War I was not the war that Isaiah 34 was talking about, which means you cannot use Isaiah 34:2 to identify 1914 as the year for anything.

Do you see how Iglesia ni Cristo must bend facts of history? What does it say? "Oh we don't look at history. We look at the Bible." But then it goes and argues history. It goes so far as to argue that in Isaiah there are references to army tanks and airplanes. Give me a break. That's not in there at all. On what biblical basis is authority in the Iglesia ni Cristo passed along? On no biblical basis. Why did Eraño Manalo become the successor of Felix Manalo? Because he was his son, that's why, not because he had any authority. Was there an election of some sort? No. It was a family concern. That's all.

I mentioned, in my opening remarks, Iglesia ni Cristo is fond of claiming that the pope is the beast of Revelation. We know that the beast of Revelation has the number 666, right? Now here is the argument. Follow this carefully. The popes have what is known as a tiara, a triple crown. The beast can be identified as a man whose name adds up to 666 or a man whose title adds up to 666. Iglesia ni Cristo says two things: first, that the title of the pope, in Latin, is "*Vicarius Filii Dei*," and second, that that title appears on the three bands of the tiara. I have in front of me a photocopy of the September 1976 issue of *Pasugo*. Here is a drawing made by the staff showing the tiara, with those words on it. This is just a pen drawing.

Does the title *Vicarius Filii Dei* add up to 666? Yes, it does. But, is it a title of the popes? Have they ever used it? No. Do you know what *Vicarius Filii Dei* means? It means "Vicar of the Son of God." Pope have never used that title. No pope ever. The official title of the pope is Vicar of Christ, not Vicar of the Son of God. We Catholics claim he is the representative on Earth of the God-man, the Messiah, not of the Second Person of the Trinity as such. The title "Vicar of Christ," in Latin, is *Vicarius Christi.* The letters don't add up to 666. So, this is the first thing that Iglesia ni Cristo has done—and it repeats this story every four issues or so in its magazine.

I showed you the picture where someone penciled in the words "*Vicarius Filii Dei*" on the tiara. Have you ever seen a good photograph of the tiara? Iglesia ni Cristo says these words are written in jewels on the tiara and that the word "*Dei*," which means "of God," is written in a hundred diamonds. Is that the case? All we have to do is turn to that September 1976 issue of *Pasugo*, to the beginning of that article, where there is a picture of Pope Paul VI, who was the last pope to wear the tiara. The picture shows that there are no words at all on the tiara.

The writers in *Pasugo* have lied again to you. Worse, they are insulting you because on one page they show you that there are no words on the tiara, and elsewhere they make a line drawing and add in the words, and they think you are too stupid to see it.

I was warned by some well-intentioned people that I shouldn't come here tonight and talk tough about the fraudulence of Iglesia ni Cristo. They said, "The Iglesia people will shout you down," but you haven't shouted me down. They said, "They will interrupt you," and you have interrupted, but not too often. They said, "They are closed-minded," and maybe some of you are. Of course, you find closed-minded people in every church, don't you? You also find open-minded people. Many of you who are members of Iglesia ni Cristo were brought up as Catholics. You probably learned next to nothing about the Catholic faith. I must conclude that because you are swallowing this nonsense that Iglesia puts out about the Catholic Church. Forget, for the moment, Iglesia's own credibility. Look at what it says against the competition. Why does it feel it must lie regularly about the Catholic Church, such as with this thing with the pope's tiara and 666?

Iglesia ni Cristo doesn't want you to know things. It doesn't want you to know the truth about the Catholic faith, about the Bible, or about your own religion. You've got to ask yourself, if that's the case, how can this possibly be of God? How can a church that has borrowed its principles from nineteenth-century Protestants and sectarians possibly be God's real Church? Thank you.

MODERATOR: We will now hear a five-minute cross-question period from the affirmative side. Brother Ventilacion.

VENTILACION: Mr. Karl Keating, I would like to ask you, in John 10:16, did not Christ say that, "I have other sheep"?

KEATING: Yes, he did, and he meant the Gentiles.

VENTILACION: Okay. Christ said that there shall be one shepherd and one flock. Who is the one shepherd?

KEATING: We all know who that is. It's Jesus Christ.

VENTILACION: It's Jesus Christ? Why did Christ say, "And there will be a flock and one shepherd"? Isn't it that Jesus Christ was already a shepherd?

KEATING: He was already the shepherd.

VENTILACION: Right. So, when he said there will be one shepherd, is he still the one shepherd, then?

KEATING: He founded his Church. He's the shepherd of it.

VENTILACION: Let me ask you another question.

KEATING: Of course, at the end of John's Gospel he also names Peter as a shepherd: "Feed my lambs, feed my sheep, feed my sheep."

VENTILACION: So, in John 10:16, is this the apostle Peter?

KEATING: No. At the end of John's Gospel. "Feed my lambs, feed my sheep, feed my sheep." That's where he gives the position of shepherd, in some sense, to Peter.

VENTILACION: That answers my question. Now, in John 13:20 Christ said, "Whosoever accepts the one that I sent, receives me." Do you believe that?

KEATING: I believe everything the Bible says.

VENTILACION: So, you believe that Christ could send another messenger, then?

KEATING: Not one from the Philippines named Manalo. No.

VENTILACION: But you believe that Christ could send a messenger?

KEATING: The messengers he sent out, two by two, were his own disciples.

VENTILACION: We believe that Brother Felix Manalo was a messenger.

KEATING: Fine. You can believe it, but it has no scriptural basis.

VENTILACION: This is the question. When he taught us that the Father is the only true God, is that a wrong teaching?

KEATING: Of course it's wrong. Jesus is God, the Holy Spirit is God, the Father is not the only God. There is one God who is three divine Persons, Father, Son, Holy Spirit.

VENTILACION: This is the question, because Father Felix Manalo taught us about the one God.

KEATING: I don't care what Manalo taught.

VENTILACION: In John 17:3, Christ is the one speaking, right?

KEATING: Read it to us.

VENTILACION: Okay. These were the words. "And this is eternal life that they may know you, the only true God." To whom did Christ address that word?

KEATING: To his Father.

VENTILACION: To the Father. Hold on. I'm not yet through.

KEATING: I'm not through answering either. I was interrupted by the audience. Will you let me finish my answer?

VENTILACION: If the Father—

KEATING: Will you let me finish my answer?

VENTILACION: Go ahead.

KEATING: What you fail to do is make a distinction between the Trinity and tritheism, three gods. We believe in one God who is in three Persons, not in three gods. Your arguments are all against three gods.

VENTILACION: I repeat, again, my question. Christ said, "The Father is the only true God." Is that wrong or right?

KEATING: There is only one God. The Father is the only true God, Jesus Christ is the only true God, the Holy Spirit is the only true God.

VENTILACION: Where in the Bible does it says that the Holy Spirit is the only true God?

KEATING: What do you think the Holy Spirit is, some force?

VENTILACION: Don't ask me, I am asking you. Where does it say in the Bible that the Holy Spirit is the only true God? What verse?

KEATING: You want those exact words?

VENTILACION: Yes.

KEATING: Just like I wanted the exact words of where the Philippines are mentioned?

VENTILACION: I'm asking you about those words, what you said. Where does it say that the Holy Spirit is the only true God? What verse?

KEATING: Those exact words are not used.

VENTILACION: Then why did you say that if that is not in the Bible?

KEATING: I didn't say that is not in the Bible. What I said is that the Bible teaches—

VENTILACION: It is in the Bible, then?

KEATING: The Bible teaches—

VENTILACION: It is in the Bible, then?

KEATING: The Bible teaches that the Father is God, that the Son is God, that the Holy Spirit is God.

VENTILACION: That is not my question. My question, Mr. Keating, is this. You said that the Holy Spirit is the only true God. If the Holy Spirit, granting—but not conceding, granting—that the Holy Spirit is the only true God, how many only true Gods do you have?

KEATING: One!

VENTILACION: One? The Father is the only true God? How do you understand the word "only"? Is there another one aside from him?

KEATING: The word "only" comes from the word "one."

VENTILACION: My question is, when Christ said that the Father is the only true God, what did he mean by the word "only"? Is there another God aside from him?

KEATING: Jesus was not saying that he was not God, or that the Holy Spirit was not God.

VENTILACION: He was teaching that the Father is the only true God, right?

KEATING: In my opening remarks I gave you all kinds of quotations proving that Jesus Christ is divine. You have not talked about any of them.

VENTILACION: You cannot answer the question.

MODERATOR: Thank you very much, gentlemen. We now go to a seven-minute rebuttal from the affirmative side. Brother Ventilacion.

VENTILACION: You know, Mr. Keating did not prove his church is, indeed, the true Church. So, during his presentation, he attacked on the concept of Jesus Christ as God or not. That is not in our discussion today in the debate. But he went into that, so I just followed him. When I asked him that when Brother Felix Manalo taught us that the Father is the only true God and is that a wrong doctrine, he said yes. He said that the Son is the only true God, and the Holy Spirit is the only true God. He admitted, also, that the Father is the only true God. So what does it mean? What Brother Felix Manalo taught to us, that the Father is the only true God, is also admitted by Mr. Karl Keating. Right, Mr. Keating?

Why is it then that the debate went to this? It is to prove which church is the true Church. I told him we can debate another time concerning if Christ is God or not or the Holy Spirit is God or not, but he forced me to do this. So I have been asking him, basing from the teachings of Christ, what did Christ say? Christ said, "The Father is the only true God." I repeat that word again. "And this is eternal life, that they may know you, the only true God." I asked him what he means by that word "only." Is there another God? He said, the Son is also the true God. The Holy Spirit is also the true God. What does he mean by the word "only"? When Christ said that the Father is the only true God, that is not placing Christ as God.

In John 17:3 Christ proclaimed, "The Father is the only true God." But after that, what did Christ mention about himself? This Brother Felix Manalo taught us, too. "And Jesus Christ, whom you have sent." Whose words are these? These are the words of Christ. Did he say that "I am also a true God?" Mr. Keating said Christ is also an only true God, but Christ did not present himself as the only true God. I challenged him again, if he could prove, from the Bible: where did Christ say that he is the only true God? Mr. Keating, I hope you hear that challenge.

Where did Christ say that "I am the only true God"? Where in the Bible did it mention that the Holy Spirit is the only true God? That's what you believe, so I ask you: how many only true Gods do you believe in? He has the Father as the only true God. He has the Son as the only true God. He has the Holy Spirit as the only true God. You have three only true Gods. I thought you believed in only one God. Now, it happens there are three only true Gods. I hope Mr. Keating can find that in the Bible.

Most of our members here were Catholics before. Brother Felix Manalo taught us that the Father is the only true God, and that is from the Bible. We accepted that Brother Felix Manalo was, indeed, a messenger of God. But the truth remains. The truth remains. The basic doctrine concerning God was already taught to us by Brother Felix Manalo. What about the apostles? When the apostles were preaching, whom did the apostles teach as the only true God? This Brother Felix Manalo also taught us.

The apostles teach that the one God is composed of three? In 1 Corinthians 8:6 I read, "Yet there is for us only one God, the Father." What did the apostles say? The apostles said, "Yet for us there is only one God." The apostles are in the true Church. Mr. Keating is teaching that the only one God is not only the Father but the Son and the Holy Spirit. It is a combination of three Gods. But the apostles said, "For us, there is only one God, and that is the Father." The apostles did not say the Father, the Son, and the Holy Spirit.

Did not Brother Felix Manalo teach us this, my beloved brethren? Yes. Therefore, the spirit of Christ and the spirit of the apostles is the same spirit that guided Brother Felix Manalo. That's why we, most of us, who were Catholics before—why did we leave the Roman Catholic Church? Because just on the basics they are already wrong. How much more on the other doctrines of the Catholic Church? That is why we could not accept that the Catholic Church is the true Church. They are the fulfillment of the apostatized church. We believe that when Christ said "I shall have other sheep" there shall be one flock, that's one Church, there shall be one shepherd. That shepherd is Brother Felix Manalo, not Jesus Christ, because Christ said, "There will be." That is in the future. Now, no matter how he will attack the personality of Brother Felix Manalo, we remain in believing that he is a messenger of God because of the teachings.

On April 18, 1915, in the *Sunday Visitor*, which was published in Huntington, Indiana, it mentions that the pope's title is *Vicarius Filii Dei*. This is according to the book *The Beast of Revelation*.

KEATING: Are you saying that's true? Are you saying that the pope's tiara has *Vicarius Filii Dei* written on it? Are you saying that?

VENTILACION: *Vicarius Filii Dei* means Vicar of God.

KEATING: I know what it means. It means Vicar of the Son of God. Is that on the pope's tiara?

VENTILACION: According to the—

KEATING: According to your knowledge, is it on there or is it not?

VENTILACION: According to what I have learned from the book *The Beast of Revelation,* in our *Sunday Visitor* they published that in—

KEATING: What you have done is you accepted, uncritically, an anti-Catholic work. You mentioned the book—

VENTILACION: It's your problem to debate with the Adventists, not with me.

KEATING: You use their argument. You admit it's wrong. Now you say, "Don't complain to me, argue with them."

VENTILACION: Question: in your book, does it say 616 or 666?

KEATING: In the ancient manuscript it has both but 666 is obviously the proper one.

VENTILACION: Which Catholic book could you show me that it is 616?

KEATING: Ancient manuscripts. Do you have any books—

VENTILACION: I'm asking you a Catholic book. Right now.

KEATING: Okay. I will give you one.

VENTILACION: The Catholic book?

KEATING: Look at Nestle's New Testament which gives the Greek. It gives a reference, in the footnote, to both numbers.

VENTILACION: I will not also believe you because you cannot show me.

MODERATOR: We will have a seven-minute rebuttal from the negative side, Mr. Keating.

KEATING: I hope you are all paying close attention to what he is doing. He refuses to answer questions straight. He admits that *Pasugo* publishes lies. He says it's not our fault because we took it from another publication. He won't go back to the original sources. I'm continually amazed at Mr. Ventilacion's apparent ignorance of what the doctrine of the Trinity means. I have never come across somebody who talks in public about the Trinity and doesn't even know its definition. He claims to have read my book and apparently other Catholic books. How come he doesn't know what the doctrine of the Trinity is? He keeps saying it means three Gods. It doesn't. Every Protestant book that talks about it, every Catholic book that talks about it, every Eastern Orthodox book that talks about it makes the distinction clearly. What's the problem with Iglesia ni Cristo? You see Iglesia's position will fall apart if it admits that the Trinity is about one God, not three Gods.

He asked me for any proof, any proof at all, that the Holy Spirit is divine. Let me cite a verse for you. Look at Acts 5. There is the story, at the beginning, of Ananias and Sapphira. Remember what they did? They sold their property and gave part of it to the common fund, but they kept back some, and they lied about it. They committed fraud. They said, "We are giving all of our property, all of the proceeds, to the Church," but they were lying. And what happened? Both of them were struck dead by God, right? Verse 5:3 says, "They defrauded the Holy Spirit." The very next verse says. "It is God, not man, that you have defrauded." Verse 3 says, you defrauded the Holy Spirit. The next verse says, it is God that you have defrauded. Therefore, the Holy

Spirit is God. All the early Christians knew that. They didn't have a problem with it.

Felix Manalo came to the U.S. and got it in his head that he would borrow from off-shoots from Protestantism such as the Jehovah's Witnesses and the Mormons. He borrowed the idea that the Holy Spirit isn't God, that Jesus isn't God. Why? Because he could go back to the Philippines preaching a new gospel, different from the one taught by the Catholic Church. Doing that, he could get a following. He wasn't out for truth. Remember the line "even if an angel should preach to you a new gospel"? Manalo claimed to be that angel from the Philippines. He used the term "angel" to describe himself as messenger. That's the false gospel, but it's not original with Manalo. He wasn't bright enough to make it up on his own. He borrowed it from others. Let me repeat verses I mentioned earlier. God the Father is called Lord of Lord and King of Kings. So is Jesus, in Revelation 17:4. God the Father is called the Alpha and the Omega. That is the designation for God. So is Jesus the Alpha and the Omega, in Revelation 1:8. Jesus uses the Father's own proper name for himself: "I Am."

What did the Jews start to do when he said that? Do you remember what follows, after John 8:58? They took up stones to kill him. Why? Because they thought he committed the ultimate blasphemy, which is to say that he was God. They wouldn't have taken up stones if he said, "Oh, I'm the image of God only, or I'm related to God, or God is my Father, the same way he's your Father." They were going to kill him, because he claimed to be God, and they knew what he was saying when he said those sacred words: "I Am."

Hebrew 1:8 addresses Christ. It says, "Thy throne, O God, is forever." That's talking to Christ, calling him God. Colossians 2:9: "In Christ the fullness of deity dwells." Complete deity in Christ. Isaiah 45:23 says, "To God the Father every knee must bend." Mr. Ventilacion pointedly ignored Philippians 2:10, which says that "to Jesus Christ every knee must bend." *Pasugo* repeatedly brings up the fact, according to it, that if you bow to something, then you worship it as God. So if you bow to Jesus, you must worship him as God, according to Iglesia's own principle.

But Mr. Ventilacion didn't bring that up, and he didn't mention what the apostle Thomas said when he put his hand into the risen Christ's side and then believed that he had risen from the dead. Thomas said, "My Lord and my God," and Jesus did not rebuke him. Jesus praised him. He said, "You're right, better, though, those that do not see and yet believe." But it's still good to believe when you see. Jesus did not say, "Oh, no, you're mistaken." Do you remember when, later on, someone came up to Peter and knelt before him on the ground, as though to worship him? Peter said, "Get up. I am just a man." That's right. Did Jesus tell that to Thomas? "I'm just a man"? No, he did not, because he's not just a man, he is God.

MODERATOR: We now go to a three-minute cross-question from the affirmative side. Brother Ventilacion.

VENTILACION: Well, your presentation was concerning Christ, so I have to go there. You said Manalo's teachings, right? You mentioned about Manalo's teachings?

KEATING: I mentioned quite a bit about Manalo.

VENTILACION: If Felix Manalo taught us from the Bible that Jesus Christ is a man, is that wrong?

KEATING: Jesus Christ is both man and God.

VENTILACION: That's not my question. My question is—

KEATING: I don't know what Manalo taught from the Bible. I know what he claims.

VENTILACION: That's what I'm saying—

KEATING: I know what Manalo claims, but that's not teaching from the Bible.

VENTILACION: You said you quoted Revelation 8:1 which, you said, says that Christ is God. Does it say in Revelation 8:1 that Christ is God?

KEATING: I said Revelation 1:8.

VENTILACION: Okay. Did Christ say "I am God" in Revelation 1:8?

KEATING: He says, "I am the alpha and the omega, the beginning and the end, sayeth the Lord, which is, which was, and which is to come, the almighty."

VENTILACION: Therefore, that is—

KEATING: Jesus is calling himself the Almighty.

VENTILACION: That is only your opinion.

KEATING: I'm reading from the text. What do you mean it's my opinion? You mean when I bring up a point up that contradicts you, you say that's my opinion, even though it's straight from the Bible?

VENTILACION: My question is this. Did Christ say in Revelation 1:8, "I am God." Answer yes or no.

KEATING: That's the meaning of it.

VENTILACION: In John 8:58 did Christ say, "I am God" or "I Am"?

KEATING: He used the proper name for God, which is I Am.

VENTILACION: Mr. Keating, I have to repeat my question, please. My question is this—

KEATING: Jesus said, "Before Abraham was, I Am."

VENTILACION: Did he say, "I am God?"

KEATING: He didn't need to because that's the name of God, I Am. That's what Moses was told. Look at Exodus 3:14. Moses was given the name of God. God said, "My name is I Am." God's name is not "I am God" but "I Am."

VENTILACION: Let's get to Thomas now. You said Thomas said to Jesus, "My Lord and my God," right?

KEATING: That's right.

VENTILACION: So you believe Thomas?

KEATING: I believe the Bible.

VENTILACION: That's not my question. My question is, do you believe Thomas when he said, "Jesus is my God?"

KEATING: I believe Thomas and Jesus, who approved of what he said.

VENTILACION: In John 20:17 did not Christ tell the Christians who is the God that they should believe? Before Thomas said, "My Lord and my God" to Christ, did not Christ tell them who is the God of the Christians?

KEATING: He says in that verse, "I am ascending to my God."

VENTILACION: Very good. Now—

KEATING: I want to finish the answer. It's not complete.

VENTILACION: I will ask from your—

KEATING: I'm not done with my answer. Why does he say that? Because he has two natures. His human nature in which he ascends to God. In his divine nature, he's already God. Your mistake is you think that every verse in the New Testament must be taken with the same sense. Some of them refer to our Lord's divine nature, some to his human nature. You ignore that distinction.

VENTILACION: This is my question. Did not Christ say he has a God?

KEATING: His human nature was created. Obviously he had a God.

VENTILACION: So, if he has a God, who is his God?

KEATING: He said, "I ascend to the Father."

VENTILACION: Is not the God of Christ also our God?

KEATING: Why are you avoiding what Thomas was saying? I thought we were talking about Thomas.

VENTILACION: Mr. Keating, you are out of order.

KEATING: I have to be out of order to get my point across to you.

VENTILACION: I'll tell you why later. Be patient.

MODERATOR: Thank you for the audience who are still here.

VENTILACION: I don't know why Mr. Keating always goes to if Jesus Christ is God or not when the topic here is to prove if the Church of Christ which appeared in the Philippines is the true Church. He did not disprove what I read. He has never disproved. Our presentation here is that Christ mentioned other sheep who will become one flock or one Church of Christ. The re-establishment of the Church happened in the year 1914.

Inasmuch as he would like to discuss Jesus Christ, let's follow him to that. He said, in Revelation 1:8, Christ is God. What if we read it, okay? "I am alpha and omega, the beginning and the ending, sayeth the Lord, which is, and which was, and which is to come, the almighty." This is not Jesus Christ. Mr. Keating said this is Jesus Christ. This is the Almighty God. Why would we believe that this is the Almighty God and not Jesus Christ? The word "Almighty" means the source of all power. He believes that too.

Let's go to the power that is of our Lord Jesus Christ. What kind of power does our Lord Jesus Christ possess? He said in Matthew 28:18, "And Jesus came and spake unto them saying all power is given unto me in heaven and in Earth." Who is the source of the power of our Lord Jesus Christ? He said, "all power is given unto me." There is a source of his power. He is not the Almighty. The Almighty does not derive his power from somebody else. Christ said, "all power is given to unto me." Where did he receive that power? In Matthew 11:27 Christ said, "All things are delivered unto me of my Father."

Now, Mr. Keating, I would like you to take note of what shall happen when the day of judgment shall come. Will you please explain your doctrine concerning equality here? They say, "The Father, the Son, and the Holy Spirit are equal." Here is what shall happen on the day of judgment. Read 1 Corinthians 15:27-28: "God put all things under his feet." Under the feet of Christ. It is clear, of course, that the words "all things" do not include God himself who puts all things under Christ. But when all things have been placed under Christ's rule, then he himself, the Son, will place himself under God.

Mr. Keating believes that the Father, the Son, and the Holy Spirit are equal. In this verse it says the Son, on the day of judgment, will place himself under God. Where is the equality doctrine now? Now, he said, why didn't you believe Thomas? Because Thomas was wrong. Why? Because when Christ told them about God, Thomas was not there. Everybody knows that Thomas is also called "the doubting apostle," right? He did not believe that Christ was resurrected. Before John 20:28, when Thomas said to Jesus "My Lord and my God," he did not hear the message of Christ.

What was Christ's message to them that Thomas was not able to know? Christ told them, "Touch me not, for I am not yet ascended to my Father. But go to my brethren and say unto them, I ascend unto my Father and your Father and to my God and your God." Very clear. It is so clear, Mr. Keating, that Christ is not the one true God. The Almighty God is the one who placed all things under Christ, and that is where Christ will go. He told the apostles, he told Mary Magdalene, "Tell the brethren that I go to my God. But he is not only my God, he's also your God." But Thomas was not able to know this. Why? Thomas, one of the Twelve, was not with them when Jesus came. He did not know. He never heard about this message. Because if he knew that Christ said, "Tell them," including Thomas, "I'm going to my God," then Thomas would not say, "My Lord and my God."

So, though Mr. Keating could not answer my question, I ask him, "Which one do you believe—Christ, who said "I'll go to my God, which is also your God," or Thomas, who said, "Jesus is my God"? Which one do you believe, Mr. Keating? Do you believe Thomas who was absent, doubting Thomas, or should you believe the Savior himself saying, "I have my God"?

Let's go back to Brother Felix Manalo. Mr. Keating criticized Brother Felix Manalo for teaching that Christ is not God. Brother Felix Manalo taught us the same teachings taught by the apostles. Why is it so hard for him to accept that Brother Felix Manalo is a messenger of God when the teachings that he taught us are all in the Bible? The apostles told us the same thing, that the Father is the only true God. That's why I am always challenging him. Show me a verse in the Bible that says Christ is the only true God. Show me in the Bible where it says the Holy Spirit is the only true God. He could not show to you any verse in the Bible where Christ said, "I am God." He could not show any verse in the Bible that says the Holy Spirit is the only true God. Therefore, the conclusion is this: this church preached by Brother Felix Manalo is the true Church from the Bible.

MODERATOR: We now have a three minute cross-question from Mr. Keating.

KEATING: You just said that it is hard for me to accept that Felix Manalo was a messenger. Apparently, it was hard for Felix Manalo to accept that he was a messenger, because he didn't preach that doctrine until 1922. My question for you is: if he was a messenger from 1914, how come he didn't know about it until 1922?

VENTILACION: How did you know that?

KEATING: Very simply. No Iglesia publication published before 1922 makes the claim. I refer to the book on the Iglesia ni Cristo by Leonard Tuggy, who's not a Catholic.

VENTILACION: Ah, Leonard Tuggy. You know Mr. Leonard Tuggy is a Baptist minister, who wrote a book against the Iglesia ni Cristo. Your foundation came from a person who wrote against the Iglesia ni Cristo.

KEATING: Do you have, in your possession tonight, any publication by Iglesia ni Cristo published before 1922 that says Manalo is a messenger?

VENTILACION: Brother Felix Manalo, since the beginning, taught this Bible. This is the Bible.

KEATING: Do you have such a publication, sir?

VENTILACION: This is the publication, if you want a publication. This is it.

KEATING: Answer the question, or have your position be condemned by all honest people in this audience.

VENTILACION: This is it. If you would like a publication, this is it, the Bible.

KEATING: Show us *Pasugo* or another magazine.

VENTILACION: *Pasugo* came out in 1939.

KEATING: I know it did.

VENTILACION: What's the problem?

KEATING: Do you have any publication, published by Iglesia ni Cristo, with you tonight, published before 1922—

VENTILACION: We do not have any *Pasugo*.

KEATING: The answer is no because there is no such publication that has that doctrine.

VENTILACION: We do not have any *Pasugo*. It came out in 1939.

KEATING: Do you have any other publication, published before 1922?

VENTILACION: There is no publication.

KEATING: Nobody published anything about Iglesia ni Cristo before 1922?

VENTILACION: Show me.

KEATING: I'm asking you. Does your church have any?

VENTILACION: That's why I told you none, because *Pasugo* came out in 1939.

KEATING: Did any Iglesia writer write anything in any publication before 1922 and say in that publication that Manalo was called as a messenger? What's your answer?

VENTILACION: We do not have any publication—

KEATING: You don't have such a thing, because there isn't one.

VENTILACION: Except the *Pasugo.* It came out in 1939.

KEATING: I said I'm not referring to *Pasugo.* I'll even accept a newspaper account from the Philippines where it says, say in 1918, that Manalo is a messenger.

MODERATOR: That ends the debate portion of our event tonight and I'd like to thank the audience for being so nice, peaceful, and quiet. I'd like to thank the two gentlemen for their being scholarly, eloquent, and sincere in presenting their sides.

So I now open the floor to questions from the audience. But when you do it, please tell who you are directing it to.

SPEAKER: My question is aimed at Mr. Ventilacion. You quoted Corinthians: "Yet there is for us only one God the Father who is the creator of all things and for whom we live, and there is only one Lord, Jesus Christ, through whom all things were created and through whom we live." Sounds to me like it's synonymous. Christ is the one through whom all things are created. God the Father is the creator of all things. So how do you explain that they are not both God when Catholics say, yes, they have those same powers?

VENTILACION: I would like you to listen to Acts 2:36, my friend. It says here, "Therefore let all the house of Israel know assuredly that God hath made the same Jesus, whom you have crucified, both Lord and Christ." There is no other person that was made Lord by God in the Christian era, except Jesus Christ.

KEATING: The questioner has a very pointed question, which, again, has been sidestepped. God the Father is called the Creator. Jesus Christ is called the one through whom all things were created. How many Creators can there be? Only one, God. There is only one God. Only God can create. A creature cannot create. A creature is created. He is not a creator. There is no way around that. "Jesus Christ, through whom all things were created." That can only mean he is the creator, and he is God. There is no other possibility, unless you are going to say that creatures can create.

SPEAKER: I would like to address this question to Mr. Keating.

SPEAKER: It is your teaching, in the Catholic Church, that the true Church was established upon the apostle Peter. Now my question is: was this same true Church ever established upon our Lord Jesus Christ? Please give me citations or verses supporting your answer.

KEATING: Mr. Ventilacion and I both gave verses regarding the establishment of the Church. My point in Matthew 16:18 was that although Jesus Christ, obviously, was the only one who could establish a church, he left behind him a visible representative on Earth who is the successor to Peter.

VENTILACION: My answer to that question is, if the Church has been built upon Peter since the beginning, then Christ, from the beginning, is not the foundation stone. You see the point? If, in Matthew 16:18, the apostle Peter became a foundation stone, then Christ did not become a foundation stone because from the start it was already the apostle Peter.

SPEAKER: I'd like to address my question to Mr. Keating. I would like him to show me a verse in the Bible where the word "Trinity" is used. And I don't want anything that tells me three in one. I want to see the word "Trinity" in the Bible.

KEATING: The word "Trinity," like the word "Philippines" and the phrase "Church of Christ," does not appear in the Bible.

SPEAKER: Tertullian, didn't he decide to use it?

KEATING: No. The first use of "Trinity" was by Theophilus of Antioch in 181. Look it up. He uses the Greek word *Trios*, which means "Trinity."

SPEAKER: But is that in the Bible? Show it to me in the Bible.

KEATING: If you are going to use that principle, then you can't say that Manalo is a messenger from the Philippines, because "Philippines" is not mentioned in the Bible.

MODERATOR: We are supposed to leave here around 10:30, so we have one more question. One more question. I'm sorry about the rest, but one more question. Thank you.

SPEAKER: First of all. I'd like to say that I am Roman Catholic, and I am very proud of my beautiful religion. I hear some laughter, but then again I hear some claps. Mr. Ventilacion, how many churches are there that call themselves the Church of Christ but are not of your same denomination and could use the same argument that they are the Church of Christ?

VENTILACION: That is probably your opinion. But this is what I can say. Not just because they use the name "Church of Christ" are they the true Church. What is to be confirmed is if their teachings are in the Bible. There is the Church of Christ here in the United States that, like the Catholics, believes in the Trinity. We don't believe that because they carry the name "Church of Christ" they are the true Church. That is not our stand, my friend. Our stand is this—

SPEAKER: Mr. Ventilacion, I believe you contradicted yourself, because earlier—

VENTILACION: You are entitled to your own opinion.

SPEAKER: No, excuse me. I'll explain why I think you contradicted yourself. Earlier you said that in Acts it talks about the Church of Christ, and you seemed to use that as proving that your church is the Church of Christ. But then you say, if other churches say they are the Church of Christ, well they can't be because—

VENTILACION: We are having a debate here.

SPEAKER: Thank you.

KEATING: This gentleman brought up a very good point. Notice Mr. Ventilacion's arguments. He says, "Ours must be the true church because it is called the Church of Christ." But when Felix Manalo came to the United States in 1919 to study, there already were churches that called themselves the Church of Christ. They came out of what is known as the Campbellite Movement from which your messenger got some of his doctrines. There are several Protestant denominations that call themselves Church of Christ and use exactly the same argument. Why aren't they the authentic church? They came before Iglesia ni Cristo. You see, Iglesia ni Cristo's argument is no good. All it is is a word game, trying to put one over on you by saying, "If this is called the Church of Christ, it must be the Church of Christ." Anybody can do that. In fact, a lot of churches have done that. Taking on a new title by itself means nothing. The man's point was well taken.

Thank You!

I hope you found this little book useful or entertaining—preferably both! If you did, please consider leaving an honest review at Amazon. It is through reviews that writers find most of their new readers.

If you have feedback about the book, I'd like to have it. You can write to me at Karl@KarlKeating.com.

The Books in This Series

The Debating Catholicism Series consists of four short books and an omnibus volume. They are:

Book 1: *The Bible Battle* (Karl Keating vs. Peter S. Ruckman)

Book 2: *High Desert Showdown* (Karl Keating vs. Jim Blackburn)

Book 3: *Tracking Down the True Church* (Karl Keating vs. Jose Ventilacion)

Book 4: *Face Off with an Ex-Priest* (Karl Keating vs. Bartholomew F. Brewer)

Omnibus Volume: *Debating Catholicism* (includes all four books above)

Other Books by Karl Keating

Apologetics the English Way

Can a reasonable case be made for Catholicism? Maybe even a compelling case? Or does the Catholic argument falter? Does it wilt before critiques from top-notch opponents? Judge for yourself. You don't have to be Catholic or even religious to relish the intellectual sparring that goes on in these pages.

Here is high-level controversial writing, culled from Karl Keating's favorite books. Each selection is a forceful exposition of Catholic truth. Most are from the 1930s, all come from English Catholics, and all are aimed at a single antagonist, with the public invited to look over the writer's shoulder. The reader can view the weaknesses and occasional mistakes even of his own champion.

These pages are filled with vivid personalities. These were men who knew the Catholic faith and could explain it to others. The individuals against whom they wrote may not have been converted—one or two were, in the long run—but any number of readers of these little-known masterpieces must have found their faith bolstered and their doubts assuaged. The issues covered in these exchanges are still discussed today—but probably nowhere in as glorious a style as here.

The New Geocentrists

Were Copernicus, Galileo, and Kepler wrong? Does Earth orbit the Sun, or does the Sun orbit Earth? For centuries, everyone thought the science was settled, but today the accepted cosmology is being challenged by writers, speakers, and movie producers who insist that science took a wrong turn in the seventeenth century. These new geocentrists claim not only that Earth is the center of our planetary system but that Earth is motionless at the very center of the universe.

They insist they have the science to back up their claims, which they buttress with evidence from the Bible and Church documents. But do they have a case? How solid is their reasoning, and how trustworthy are they as interpreters of science and theology?

The New Geocentrists examines the backgrounds, personalities, and arguments of the people involved in what they believe is a revolutionary movement, one that will overthrow the existing cosmological order and, as a consequence, change everyone's perception of the status of mankind.

No Apology

Karl Keating has been a Catholic apologist for nearly four decades. In these pages he shares some of his own experiences and some stories from times past. He writes about how to do apologetics and how not to. He defends the very idea of apologetics against a theologian who thinks apologetics is passé. He looks at how the faith is promoted through beauty and through suffering. He takes you from his own backyard to such distant times and places as fifth-century Jerusalem and sixteenth-century Japan.

Anti-Catholic Junk Food

You are what you eat. That is as true of the mind as of the body. Eat enough greasy food, and your silhouette will betray your culinary preferences. Give credence to enough greasy ideas, and your mind will be as flabby as your waistline. This book looks at eight examples of religious junk food, things that have come across Karl Keating's desk during his career as a Catholic apologist. You likely will find these morsels unconvincing and unpalatable, as you should. The problem is that plenty of people—including people on your block—consider such stuff to be intellectual high cuisine.

Jeremiah's Lament

For many, the best way to reach an understanding of the Catholic Church is to see how other people misunderstand it. This book is full of misunderstandings.

The people quoted in these pages came to their confusions in various ways. Sometimes it was by reading the wrong books or by failing to read the right books. Sometimes it was a matter of heredity, with prejudices passed down from father to son and from mother to daughter. At other times errors were imbibed at the foot of the pulpit, in the university lecture hall, or from door-to-door missionaries.

Whatever their origin, misunderstandings are misunderstandings. They should be recognized for what they are and set aside, even if that means a break from personal habit or family tradition. More than a century ago, Pope Leo XIII noted that there is nothing so salutary as to understand the world as it really is. That is true particularly of the Church that Christ established because to misunderstand her is to misunderstand him.

How to Fail at Hiking Mt. Whitney

Often, the best way to succeed at something is to learn how to fail at it—and then to avoid the things that lead to failure. There are books that tell you how to succeed at hiking Mt. Whitney. This book helps you *not* to fail by showing you what *not* to do, from the moment you start planning your trip to the moment you reach the summit.

You learn what gear not to buy and not to take, how to maximize your chances of getting a hiking permit (don't apply for the wrong days of the week!), how to prepare yourself physically without over-preparing, how to avoid being laid low by altitude or weather problems, how not to take too much food or water—or too little. You even discover how to shave a mile off the trip by using little-known shortcuts that can make the difference between reaching the summit and reaching exhaustion.

Most people who depart the Mt. Whitney trailhead fail to reach the top. Some fail because of things entirely beyond their control, but many fail because of insufficient preparation, false expectations, and basic errors of judgment. Their mistakes can come at the beginning (such as failing to get a hiking permit), during the preparation stage (such as being induced to buy "bombproof" gear), or during the hike (such as not heeding bodily warning signs).

Through engaging stories of his own and others' failures, Karl Keating shows you how to fail—and therefore how to succeed—at hiking the tallest peak in the 48 contiguous states.

About Karl Keating

Karl Keating holds advanced degrees in theology and law (University of San Diego) plus an honorary doctor of laws degree (Ave Maria University). He founded Catholic Answers, the English-speaking world's largest lay-run Catholic apologetics organization. His best-known books are *Catholicism and Fundamentalism* (nearly a quarter-million paperback copies sold) and *What Catholics Really Believe* (about half that many sold). His avocations include hiking, studying languages, and playing the baroque mandolino. He lives in San Diego. You can follow him at his author website and on Facebook:

KarlKeating.com
Facebook.com/KarlKeatingBooks